MARKETPLACE PRAYERS:

Navigating The Workplace

Nori Moore

Copyright © 2021

All rights reserved.

No part of this book may be reproduced, stored in a retrieval system, or transmitted in any form or by any means, electronic, mechanical, photocopying, recording, scanning, or otherwise, without the prior written permission of the publisher.

Disclaimer

All Biblical verses are italicized and taken from the several versions of the Holy Bible as indicated.

Every material contained in this book is provided for educational and informational purposes only.

No responsibility can be taken for any results or outcomes resulting from the use of this material.

TABLE OF CONTENTS

INTRODUCTION **5**

CHAPTER ONE **12**
  FORGIVENESS OF SIN 12
  PERSONAL PRAYER OF FORGIVENESS OF SIN 20
  PRAYER OF FORGIVENESS OF SIN FOR FOUNDERS OWNERS SUPERVISOR AND COWORKERS 22

CHAPTER TWO **25**
  PUTTING GOD FIRST 25

CHAPTER THREE **35**
  COMMITTING YOUR WORK TO GOD 35
  PRAYER TO REQUEST GOD'S HELP 41

CHAPTER FOUR **48**
  SEEKING GOD'S REWARD 48
  PRAYER FOR YOUR ORGANIZATION 54

CHAPTER FIVE **56**
  INTERCEDING FOR PEOPLE IN AUTHORITY 56
  PRAYER FOR YOUR SUPERVISORS 59

CHAPTER SIX **61**
  INTERCEDING FOR YOUR COWORKERS . 61
  PRAYER FOR COWORKERS 64

CHAPTER SEVEN **66**

MAINTAINING ETHICS IN THE MARKETPLACE 66

PRAYER FOR UPHOLDING ETHICS: 72

CHAPTER EIGHT 74

COMPETITION IN MARKETPLACE 74

CHAPTER NINE 87

MANIFESTATION OF GOD'S GLORY 87

CHAPTER TEN 96

COMMANDING GOD'S FAVOR 96

CHAPTER ELEVEN 100

PRAYING FOR PROMOTION 100

PRAYER FOR PROMOTION AND INCREASE 106

CHAPTER TWELVE 108

EFFECTIVE PRAYER LIST FOR THE MARKETPLACE 108

ABOUT THE AUTHOR 113

NORI MOORE..113

INTRODUCTION

As Christians, we seek the face of God in prayers for different reasons. For some, we are conscious that leaving everything in His hands is the only way to achieve everything we set our hearts to. We talk to God to help us in our day-to-day activities, our family, our career, our business, and our workplace, with the realization that little or nothing is achievable without His presence. We can easily tell when our career, business, or marketplace is thriving by how much of God's grace, mercy, peace, and favor is in the atmosphere.

Interestingly, the nature of a given workplace is interacting daily with others. This requires wisdom to know when to respond, to react, to encourage, to persuade, and in some cases, to condone excesses. Sometimes, your colleagues, supervisors, or coworkers may exhibit a carefree attitude that perpetually frustrates you. Still, as a Christian – you cannot allow this attitude to manifest toward them. You have a greater role to play now by praying for them. Because you are the light of the world, you have to ask God for help, pray for them and ask for the required strength to pull through. Start each day with prayers, seeking the Holy Spirit to guide, teach and lead you.

In this book, you will learn the myriads of workplace prayers that can position you better and help you and your organization achieve its goals. Moses writes in the Old Testament; *"The Lord Himself goes before you and will be with you; He will never leave you nor forsake you. Do not be afraid; do not be discouraged"* Deuteronomy 31:8 (KJV).

Why do you need prayers in your life?

We must ask and answer the question; why do you need prayers in your life? When we are praying or meditating, we are communicating with God. We are sharing our deepest fears and desires with Him. In doing so, we are also asking Him for His help and protection over us as we move through our lives. The experience of having prayers answered or received has a powerful impact on us as individuals and as a whole.

A life without prayers would be one of very little joy and abundance. Because of the power of prayer, we can move forward in life and accomplish all that is asked of us. So, you need to have prayers in your life because you want to experience the blessings of having them answered by those who care.

It is easy to see how the practice of prayer has endured throughout the centuries. Throughout the centuries, people have faced many obstacles and problems. Sometimes, it would be as simple as being separated from family. At other times, it would be as significant as being wiped out of the world altogether.

"Be careful for nothing, but in everything by prayer and supplication with thanksgiving let your requests be made known unto God." - Philippians 4:6

So, why do we need to enter into this world and endure? Why don't we just accept the obstacles that come our way and go on with our lives? If this was not the case, then there would be very few people in this world.

Because we have a purpose in life, we understand what we are here to do. We have a mission, and that is to understand the world and ourselves. We have come into this world to find peace, joy, and happiness. We have also come to learn that many things can help us achieve these things. Why do we need to do so much to understand and make a difference in this world? We are given a short time to live in the flesh, and if we are not careful, we will waste our lives.

We also need to have these thoughts and feelings because we should, as believers believe that we have been given instructions on how to live. We are given the opportunity to choose which lessons we are going to learn; however, each of us also can choose which lessons we are not going to learn. This is one of the reasons why we need to pray for guidance.

Prayers are given to understand what it is that we are here to do. It is answered, and we find the strength and knowledge to carry on. Those who have found that strength and knowledge to carry on have found a purpose in life. They have reasons for living; they understand that a life-long journey and finding purpose are important.

Finally, we have discovered that those with a clear mind have an easier time making decisions; they do not have doubts. Those with doubt do not take the time to think about their actions. Having a clear mind also helps us to reach conclusions. This has been known all along by those who have made it; they understand that some hard truths come with living. Why do you need to do so many things in life? What would you have to lose if you took a few minutes to reflect?

We understand that, as humans, we do not want to believe everything at first. We want to question those who offer us answers and do our own research. That is how we get to the point where we can conclude if the answer makes sense to us or not.

You need to have spiritual practices in your life to bring you closer to God. He is closer than you think, and he can show you what it means to have a purpose in life. Sometimes you may not feel like you have found your purpose, but you never know until you ask. Until then, you have a workable answer for why you need prayer in your life.

God gave us a reason why He created us, and we need to use that reason every day. If we did not find reasons for why we have been given certain things in life, we would not be in the position we are in today. If we only found a reason once, why would we need to find it again for our life? Prayers are an important part of the Christian faith, and it is a good idea to learn how to give them daily.

God's promise to answer every prayer according to His grace, love, faithfulness and infinite power is still valid. As Christians, what we need is to understand the strategic principles and follow them accordingly. With an attitude of confidence and solid assurance that God can do more than we ask or imagine, according to His will, you are admitting your deficiency as human and putting God first - trusting Him as the miracle-working God and that with Him on your side, you can win.

So what do you want in your marketplace? Do you want the miraculous to be unleashed or the strength and wisdom to overcome challenges and discouragement? Are you particularly concerned about changing your organization's outlook and its people, bringing them to God, and witnessing His mighty working power in your workplace?

This book's pages will show you specific techniques for praying for your organization, the workers, and the supervisors. If you are reading this book because you desire to see the hand of the Lord in your workplace or whatever mountain you are assigned to in the marketplace, I sincerely applaud you.

Let's proceed then, shall we?

CHAPTER ONE

FORGIVENESS OF SIN

"If I regard iniquity in my heart, the Lord will not hear me."

Psalm 66:18 (KJV)

Many a time, we desire to see the hand of God in different aspects of our life. Unfortunately, we are set back by sin and have failed to repent of the things that have blocked our access to heaven. The truth is this - sin separates us from God. It creates an unnecessary barrier and disconnects us from the deserved blessing and inheritance of our Father. Think about every ill-feeling, thought, or action that you have exhibited in your workplace. Ask God to remove those stains and, ultimately, the stench from your heart so you can position your heart perfectly before God and begin to exude His grace.

In the book of Acts, the church calls for forgiveness of all their sins. God promises to heal those who have been injured and to deliver them from their sins. The idea is that once we are healed, we can walk gracefully into our future lives with less fear of offending others.

This forgiveness does not come easily or without work. It takes work to fully understand and gain access to God's mercy, then forgives all our sins.

The book of 2 Chronicles 7:14 also stresses that *"If my people, which are called by my name, shall humble themselves, and pray, and seek my face, and turn from their wicked ways; then will I hear from heaven, and will forgive their sin, and will heal their land."*

However, people forget, and sometimes deliberately, are led away from the promises of forgiveness. When God promises forgiveness to someone, it means that the sinner has repented and allowed God the opportunity to heal them by pouring out his whole heart before God. When we allow ourselves to do this, God will certainly heal us because we have yielded to the power of the spirit and not our flesh. We have placed too much trust in material and earthly things in nature and have forgotten God.

"[16] Let me emphasize this: As you yield to the dynamic life and power of the Holy Spirit, you will abandon the cravings of your self-life [17] When your self-life craves the things that offend the Holy Spirit, you hinder him from living free within you! And the Holy Spirit's intense cravings hinder your self-life from

dominating you! So then, the two incompatible and conflicting forces within you are your self-life of the flesh and the new creation life of the Spirit. ⁸*But when you yield to the life of the Spirit, you will no longer be living under the law, but soaring above it!"* Galatians 5:16-18 TPT

The reason for forgiveness is that God wants people to remember that he is God and to keep in mind the grace he has given us. There is a lot of guilt that we have accumulated throughout our lifetime. This has caused all sorts of evil to manifest in our lives. God does not want this to happen and has ordained that forgiveness must occur for everything to work out the right way.

It is not enough to simply confess our guilt and say that we know it is wrong. We must go further and offer an action plan on how God is going to help us. There is no magic formula when it comes to forgiveness. God does not need a magic wand to make everything right again. We simply need to humble ourselves before God and ask forgiveness for the hurt that we inflicted upon others. We must accept the fact that we have sinned and ask forgiveness for the hurt that was inflicted.

Many verses in the Bible show us what it means to be forgiven. Forgiving is more than just a good deed done to appease God. It is actually a process that takes place within us. We have to continually move forward until we realize that we can never go back and change what someone else has done to us.

People tend to look at forgiveness as being temporary. They want God to just forgive them so they can move on with their life. It's easy to see why people feel this way, but it is far from the truth. Those who have gone through forgiveness will tell you that the healing process actually brings peace, joy, and happiness into their life. It lifts burdens from their shoulders and allows them to experience the life they deserve.

God does not require us to forgive every single individual who does something wrong to Him; that was why he laid emphasis in Luke 6:37, "***Judge not, and ye shall not be judged: condemn not, and ye shall not be condemned: forgive, and ye shall be forgiven.***"

There's going to always be someone who does things that we don't like or approve of. That's just part of life, and we are expected to sometimes act on those things that we disagree with. The difference here is that we no longer argue back when someone behaves badly towards us. Instead, we simply forgive and turn around and face them when they come back to haunt us.

As you can see, forgiveness is not only about what somebody else did to you but also what God did for you. Forgiving is simply a new perspective in life. We are no longer have to fight or battle with sin. Jesus died for this cause. People everywhere are starting to realize that they have a choice and can choose to walk straight up to God and ask for forgiveness instead of just burying their heads in the sand and hoping that God will just forget about them.

Does sin hinder prayers? The answer is "Yes!". Sin hinders the prayers of the people of God, and several scriptures in the Bible confirm this. Prophet Isaiah wrote in Isaiah 59:2 (KJV); ***"But your iniquities have separated between you and your God, and your sins have hidden his face from you,*** *that he will not hear.*" As much and readily as God would like to attend to the requests of His people, sin is the only barrier to answered prayers. Yet God is merciful and gracious to hear us and listen to our requests.

God is interested in us abhorring evil and clinging to only the good, pursuing godliness, faith, love, patience, gentleness. Paul's protégé, Timothy, writes in I Timothy 6:11 (KJV) that we should follow after righteousness. Therefore, we must return and repent from every sin. Repentance will break the yoke of unanswered prayers since it involves deciding to perform God's statutes and commandments. You also have to strive to keep your thoughts pure and only according to the word of God.

In essence, an effective prayer life requires a deliberate effort, with the help of God, to rid yourself of all hindrances. If you notice that your prayers are not getting the right answers or not yielding as many results as you expect, it could be the result of sin.

"When the heaven is shut up, and there is no rain, because they have sinned against thee; yet if they pray toward this place, and confess thy name, and turn from their sin when thou dost afflict them; Then hear thou from heaven, and forgive the sin of thy servants, and of thy people Israel, when thou hast taught them the good way, wherein they should walk; and send rain upon thy land, which thou hast given unto thy people for an inheritance."
-2 Chronicles 6:26-27 (KJV)

Repentance deals with your heart and sight. As we move forward, you must position your heart correctly before the Father if you desire to be effective. Take some time today to release and repent for every ill-feeling, thought, and action that you have personally committed on your job. Ask God to remove the stains and the stench from your heart regarding your workplace and those around you. To repent means, turn away from.

Total submission and acknowledgment of your fallibility will bring you up to speed to getting proportionate answers to your prayers. As we proceed, I will address certain areas from which you must turn away to experience the manifestation of the mighty hand of God in your workplace. As I personally view my own life and the lives of those close to me, I was able to create a list of areas that we must consistently repent from, especially those involving our colleagues and coworkers in faithlessness, unforgiveness, idolatry, malice, jealousy, discrimination, lack of reconciliation, bitterness, discontentment, complacency, racism, prayerlessness, pride, arrogance. These are not all, but these are the majority of the negative things which dwell in our hearts and from which we must repent.

I believe that the glory of the Lord belongs in the marketplace. The Father is looking to move through someone that could intercede for the workplace. Still, the prayer's effectiveness depends on how frequently you adhere to God's words and instructions. We must be cleansed; there must be a washing away of old that we may receive the new. It is important to note that every great move of God starts with a call to His people to pray, and that means there must be someone willing to yield themselves to intercede. Are you willing to be the intercessor that will cause a holy rumbling in your workplace?

PERSONAL PRAYER OF FORGIVENESS OF SIN

Heavenly Father, thank you for your faithfulness and long-suffering toward me. Father, I repent of my ignorance and the prejudiced mindset I have demonstrated on my job.

Forgive me for being close-minded and, at times, being unthoughtful, unloving, and without compassion for others. Forgive me for being short-tempered, rude, and distant. I acknowledge my sins before you. I make a conscious decision to openly repent and turn from all my negative actions, thoughts, and feelings that have displeased you and have been a source of sadness to others.

I pray that those I have hurt, offended, or discouraged will be healed, delivered, and restored in Jesus' mighty name. I thank you that you are faithful to forgive me of my sins and to cast them into the sea of forgetfulness, never remembering them again.

May I be faithful to walk in the new mindset, conscious of those around me, and be a true example of you in Jesus' name, I pray. Amen.

PRAYER OF FORGIVENESS OF SIN FOR FOUNDERS OWNERS SUPERVISOR AND COWORKERS

Heavenly Father, I pray on behalf of the founders, owners, supervisors, and coworkers; may their sins be forgiven. I repent from every contrary belief against your will and existence. I repent of every evil spoken word against your name and the ignorance of their mocking, for they truly do not know what they are doing! Forgive their sins of idolatry.

Father, I ask that you not turn away your heart but draw them into your arms that they might truly understand the depth, width, and height of your love for them. Father, forgive them of their pride and arrogance but visit them in your mercy.

May your name be known among them. I pray, Father, that they will be counted as your own. I pray that the glory of the Lord will fall upon them. Father, I pray that their hearts will be changed forever, and their knees will only bow to you, and their tongues confess your name alone. Father, I pray that the glory of the

Lord will consume their families and overtake their generations to come in the mighty name of Jesus. Amen.

REFLECTIONS/NOTES

CHAPTER TWO

PUTTING GOD FIRST

"But seek ye first the kingdom of God and its righteousness; and all these things shall be added unto you."

- Matthew 6: 33 (KJV)

There is no substitute for this – we must learn to acknowledge God in every aspect of our lives, in our home, in our occupation, and in our marketplace - because it determines how much of Him we also experience and enjoys. God holds a special place in our lives as our maker, and as such, we must never cease to allow Him the mantle.

First of all, putting God first in all you do means putting God first in everything you do. This includes how you treat people, where you work, what you are saying, and what you are doing. Yes, you hear me right, you heard me right. If you are willing to put God first in everything you do, you will become a very successful person; and you know what? You will see things differently as an outcome because you will always put God first.

Why would you want to put God first in everything you do? Because He is the one who created the universe, and He is the one who guides you through the journey. If you really want to become successful and reach success, you must believe that God is the one who guides and enables you. This is what it really means when God is said to be our helper and our provider.

"There hath no temptation taken you but such as is common to man: but God [is] faithful, who will not suffer you to be tempted above that ye are able; but will with the temptation also make a way to escape, that ye may be able to bear [it]."

- 1 Corinthians 10:13

Do you see what this means? It's pretty simple, actually. There is no way for you to succeed unless you believe there is a higher power than yourself helping you along the way. So, in other words, you must first get your hand to the wheel, and you can't do that without first believing there is a super-power directing and enabling you. So, basically, you don't have any chance unless you start to believe there is something bigger than yourself guiding you. When you get your hand onto the wheel, then you can go anywhere you want and accomplish anything you want.

Is that being honest with yourself or playing a little hardball with Him? Regardless of what you decide to do about this, you need to understand that you need to put God first in everything you do. This includes how you think and how you act. For example, if you're afraid of taking action, you won't succeed. If you are afraid of looking dumb, you won't accomplish anything that way either.

It's important to understand that just because I am telling you to put God first in all you do, doesn't mean that you should only do good. Works alone won't save you. You must be totally dependent upon the Holy Spirit. It simply means that you must become a totally independent person and stop thinking and acting according to others' wants and desires. You are your own individual and should live according to your will alone. If you truly want to do something in life and are afraid of failing, you won't be able to accomplish much.

You may feel like giving up, but nothing will come out of quitting on yourself.

So, as I said before, you have to put God first in all you do. The reason why this is important is that we must understand how incredible and unique He is. No other person can do or accomplish what He can. You should treat Him as your Father and trust and obey Him completely because, according to the Bible, He will never leave you nor forsake you. Still, you are to honor and obey Him always.

"I can do all things through Christ which strengtheneth me." - Philippians 4:13

So, it should be pretty obvious by now that putting God first in all you do is the way to go. You shouldn't just blindly follow Him and do things because someone else said it was a good thing to do. It is your responsibility to follow Him, lead His children, and then take the gospel to the entire world. He gave us His son Jesus Christ, and He is the one we must follow to have eternal life. If you truly want to follow Him, then you will accomplish anything you set out to do.

The extent to which we acknowledge God in our lives determines the extent to which we see him at work in our lives, homes, organization, and our environment. We must never cease to give Him (God) the place He ought to hold in our lives as this can be dangerous and detrimental just as is said in Romans 1:28 (KJV) *"And even as they did not like to retain God in their knowledge, God gave them over to a reprobate mind, to do those things which are not convenient."*

Do you want to get the best out of your workplace? The principle is straightforward - you have to acknowledge the place of God, which will ultimately help you in interacting with others appropriately. Given His guidance, you can be sure of doing the right thing and following the right path. We go about our business at work with our own direction so many times without allowing the Holy Spirit to lead. It is a dangerous thing to do.

In Exodus 32, the children of Israel ignored God's direction and refused to follow His statutes. They suffered the consequences as they were led to the worst places; this brought about some of them' death.

Thinking you can do things on your own and all by yourself without God has grave consequences. We must acknowledge Him in all our doings. King Solomon pencils this perfectly in Proverbs 3:5-6 (KJV), *"Trust in the LORD with all thine heart; and lean not unto thine own understanding. In all thy ways acknowledge him, and he shall direct thy paths."* Trusting Him with your whole heart demonstrates that you are His and are willing to commit yourself to His will at all times. Unwavering pursuit of God and the things of the Kingdom implies that we love Him and are ready to partake in the blessings and promises with which he established the earth. *"And God blessed them, saying, be fruitful, and multiply, and fill the waters in the seas, and let fowl multiply in the earth."* Genesis 1:28 (KJV).

Your workplace should have an undeniable fragrance of God therein. His presence in your workplace should be known, and you are the carrier of that fragrance. But it is through your intimacy, deep moments of prayer, and worship with the Father that you become a carrier of Heaven's aroma.

Before this time, if you have been experiencing bad days or tragic incidents in your workplace, start today by acknowledging God and sharing the knowledge of Him during your free time (breaks/lunch periods), singing, and making melodies in your heart towards Him. Have a consistent fellowship with Him, and in little or no time, you will begin to see things work in your favor. Make it a habit to fellowship with Him even when you step out to use the restroom. Suppose you had/have colleagues who disliked you for no particular reason. In that case, they will begin to like you simply because you carry the presence of God; with his presence comes love. Remember, in the presence of God, there is fullness of joy. His presence doesn't harbor hatred, but it instead will bring righteousness and peace. Wouldn't you rather have an environment filled with the goodness of God than for you to dwell in an environment of hatred and sadness?

"There is a way which seemeth right unto a man, but the end thereof are the ways of death." -Proverbs 14:12 (KJV)

As those standing and acting as His representatives here on earth, we have to put God first, honor Him and acknowledge Him in all our ways, even in the workplace. Our stands for God and things of the Kingdom of God aren't supposed to be only in the church. We shouldn't be known for our stand in God only in the church. The church is supposed to be our place or recharging and refreshing. The external environment, like our workplaces, ought to be our locations of testing and shining in God. We ought to bring forth His light to all that come in contact with us. Our lives ought to reflect Him, the difference between we who are within the Kingdom of Light and those without ought to be clear, for we are the light of the world, a people who have been called forth to show forth His goodness and righteousness in all that has to do with us.

As a Christian, you represent God here on earth – you are the salt of the world. Your responsibility must not be limited to the church alone. Beam the light of the gospel to everyone you come in contact with. As long as you put Him first, honor him, and acknowledge Him in all your ways, your life will reflect God even in the workplace.

Remember Matthew 5:14 (KJV) -"*Ye are the light of the world. A city that is set on a hill cannot be hid.*"

REFLECTIONS/NOTES

CHAPTER THREE
COMMITTING YOUR WORK TO GOD

"Fear thou not, for I am with thee: be not dismayed; for I am thy God: I will strengthen thee; yea, I will help thee; yea, I will uphold thee with the right hand of my righteousness."

– Isaiah 41:10 (KJV)

The Almighty God knows what each of us needs. He is also able to provide all of these needs according to His riches in glory in Christ Jesus. It is the Father's heart for us to seek first the Kingdom of God and his righteousness. To enjoy the avalanche of these blessings, we have a responsibility to follow the principles of seeking His righteousness. If you have your heart and mind fixed on God to know His will for your life, then you can be sure He will meet every need. The problem is that often we are fond of relying on our own wisdom rather than seeking His face. God helped Moses by revealing His ways to Him. *"He made known his ways unto Moses, his acts unto the children of Israel."* Psalm 103:7 (KJV).

Oh! that we might seek the wisdom, knowledge, and understanding of our Father. May our hearts yearn to commune with him, and may we desire a deeper relationship with him. God's assistance is an automatic response to our relationship. He is a good shepherd. He is an awesome father!

When you commit your ways and work to God, you will find that nothing can ever stop you from reaching your goals. God has unlimited resources and knows all the answers. If you truly want to work with Him and find success in your life, you need to be willing to commit your ways and be willing to follow God's directions. You need to follow what He wants for you and for your life. It will be hard at first, but if you truly want to follow God's ways, you will accomplish anything.

Many people want to follow the Lord's ways, but they have a hard time doing so because they are not willing to make a change in their life and take action. You have to be willing to change your life, even if you think it is not worth it. This is how you gain victory over your enemies.

Sometimes you will find that your life has changed dramatically for the better when you follow God's ways. Maybe you were not very religious as a child, but now you have found your life to be a joy and a promise. Maybe you used to be a salesman or a business person, but now you work with the poor instead. Maybe you were not very athletic as a child, but now you play volleyball and are on the swim team.

Whatever you are currently working with or trying to accomplish is the right path for you to follow. If you are not accomplishing anything, change that. Many times, people are not seeing the vision they have for their life. They are just working with the things that God has given them. If you are not accomplishing the goals you have set forth for yourself, then it is time to look for someone else to do this work.

Many times, people only think about how much money they have saved for their life, but never commit to saving money for the things that they want in their life. God wants you to enjoy things in your life and to have enough money saved to live the life that He wants you to live. When you commit your ways and work to God, you will soon find that your life changes dramatically, and you live the life you have always dreamed of.

If you are not accomplishing the goals you have set forth for your life, begin finding other ways to achieve your goals. The Lord knows what He is doing, and He can show you what you need to do. Sometimes it will be a simple task such as switching to a healthier diet or even changing your wardrobe. Sometimes, though, it may be more difficult. You may want to go back to school and change your major. It is up to you to work with the Lord to achieve these goals.

There are so many different opportunities out there for people to help others. Once you realize that you are not putting your needs before His, you will be able to get to work in His time. There are people out there who would like to have a different job or be in a different field. These are the types of people who might seek the help of someone who has been where they are and have done what they need to do to make their life better.

These are just a few examples of how you can live differently if you really want to. If you have been searching for a better life, start by committing your ways and works to God. You will find that life changes immediately, and you will feel like you have accomplished so much more than you ever thought was possible. You will never look at life the same again.

God's need in all ramifications of our lives is undeniable. When He is involved in every aspect of your life, He makes your life seem like a dreamland playing out in reality. You must know that God is constant at all times, and we are the seeming variables.

Having a deeper relationship with God will inevitably make us enjoy His assistance, which is an automatic response that he is a good shepherd and an awesome father. If you involve God in all areas of your life, He assures you of living a life full of His glory. Our God is unchanging. Every other thing changes and this is why He is called the I AM THAT I AM. Hence, it is His will to meet every need- financial and otherwise. He is our present help in times of need – especially for guidance, development, associations, relationships, and others. Given the opportunity to take charge, God is ready to provide a tremendous amount of assistance in all we do.

Enough of living our lives as if God does not exist. "*Behold, I stand at the door, and knock: if any man hears my voice, and open the door, I will come into him, and will sup with him, and he with me.*" Revelations 3:20 (KJV). He wants to be of total assistance, but we must let Him. One of the reasons we think God is not helping us enough is because we rely on ourselves too often. Therefore, it is difficult to overcome the numerous challenges in your workplace since we try to crack the solutions all by ourselves. So, what should you do? You have to turn to Him with humility in your heart, seeking His guidance and leading.

We live our lives in our workplaces in total abandonment of God; we go through challenges all week thinking of solutions to various challenges, cracking our brains but neglecting the one who has the solution to all challenges that can and will ever come up.

He is also willing to draw near unto us. Jeremiah 29:13 (KJV) says, "*And ye shall seek me, and find me, when ye shall search for me with all your heart.*" Those who genuinely seek God will find Him. Involve Him in the affairs of your life, leaving nothing behind. Give God full access to move mightily in your workplace, and it is unimaginable how much assistance you can get in return. You need to consciously let God in. He is a perfect gentleman; he would not come in when not invited, he would not stay when His presence is being rejected and taken for granted. God doesn't impose Himself on individuals regardless of how much He desires to be involved in their lives. You need to do this consciously, not assuming that He would come into your workplace and environment by proxy.

PRAYER TO REQUEST GOD'S HELP

Prayer points for the Lord can help you get in touch with him if you're having a rough time. These are places where you can pray and where he can be found. If you don't have any of these, you may be missing out on the most important part of your relationship with him.

Millions have no idea just where to begin looking for prayer points for God's help.

If you're interested in finding a way to connect with him, consider using prayer points. This is a powerful way to connect with him. Many people continue going to church in hopes of hearing what they need to say. They don't really pay attention to where their prayer efforts are taking them. You can change that very quickly.

You may already have some prayer points that you use daily. If so, use those prayer points to keep in contact with God. It can help you feel a little less alone in this extremely personal relationship with the Lord.

There are also many resources available to help you find your prayer points. You can look on the internet, in books, or even ask other Christians for advice. There are even resources designed specifically for people in your church who need help. You're never alone when you're praying for your relationship with God, and you shouldn't be.

One thing you should understand is that you should never think that you're weird for praying to the Lord. Some people may think that you're weak for praying, but this simply isn't true.

So, while there may be times when you don't feel up to it physically, you can easily find some peace in prayer by working through these points. Sometimes, all you need to do is set your hands to the praying heart and let the answers come to you. Other times, you may need more encouragement. In those situations, prayer points can help to get you on your way.

You may be surprised to find out that there are so many resources available to you. They can help you find hundreds of prayer points to bring you closer to the Lord every day. It can be overwhelming to try and figure everything out on your own. That's why these great websites and books are created. They provide helpful tips and information to make prayer a lot easier to do.

Don't let the idea that there may be hundreds of prayer points confuse you. Once you start looking at them and putting them into place, you'll find that they make a huge difference in how you pray. You can learn a lot from these resources. You'll be able to grow in wisdom and know what to do when you're faced with a tough situation or have a big question.

Now that you've taken the time to look at these things, you may be wondering when you should use them. This is really personal. If you're not already doing it, then now would be a perfect time. When you have questions about your faith or about praying, you'll be able to find the answers using these resources, the bible and reputable books on prayer and faith. You may even find something that you never even thought about before. It could completely change the way you approach prayer and how you approach life in general.

Prayer is a very important part of any life. When you're in prayer, you're given a chance to put things into perspective. If you're feeling stressed out, you can find some peace by simply sitting down for a few minutes and praying. There are plenty of people who find it difficult to pray. Prayer is something that can help you make it through life and to be strong in all situations.

It might seem like an extra thing to do, but you don't have to spend hours just trying to figure out where your prayer points are. You'll be able to find them with ease if you just take the time to look. The whole point of this process is to bring you closer to God. The more you grow in your relationship with Him, the more you'll find yourself praying.

The most important thing is to remember that you shouldn't set your prayer points when you think you're down. If you feel like you need to do something, do it, but don't push it on yourself. You don't want to force it on yourself when you're not ready. Instead, just quietly do it when it fits and pray for what you need; don't worry about any prayer points at that time. That's the best way to go about it.

Prayer

Father, I thank you for today. Thank you for how far I have come in this journey of life and in my workplace. Thank you for being the Lord and Savior over my life. Thank you, Father, for the finished work of Christ on the cross of Calvary for me and for my sins.

I pray, Father, that from today henceforth, your presence be made known in my workplace. I pray that in my life, I would enjoy your divine guidance and your divine provision. You are my ever-present help in times of need. I commit my entire self and work into your hands.

Lead me, guide me and teach me. I will never be stranded- not of money, not of fresh ideas. Thank you, Father, for my light shall break forth because you are at work in my life in Jesus' name. Amen.

REFLECTIONS/NOTES

CHAPTER FOUR
SEEKING GOD'S REWARD

"The man who plants and the man who waters have one purpose, and each will be rewarded according to his own labor. For we are God's fellow workers, you are God's field, God's building."

– 1 Corinthians 3:8-9 (KJV)

In our workplace, we have a duty and responsibility to intercede for our organization. The extent to which you stand in the gap, interceding for your organization or company determines to an extent what good you get from the organization or company. The level of integrity exhibited by the organization goes a long way in establishing the right perception in their customers' hearts and those with which they deal with.

Some people think that this is something that must be learned on one's own merit. This could be true, as some people have been born into the right position and given God's promise and then never feel they need to work for it. Other people think that the answer to seeking God's reward can only be found in a direct experience. If you seek God's favor and give Him your full attention, you may get His favor and find a way of getting what you want from Him.

Some people think that asking how to seek God's favor is an impossible thing. They might tell you that a person can't have any control over what happens to him or her when God gives them His divine promises. This is not true. Others may tell you that you must work to receive the favor of God.

These two views are incorrect. You do not have to work for it to receive His favor. The truth is that some people think that they must work for it all the time, but that isn't true either because the more you focus on the Lord and pray, the more He will draw you closer to Him. His favor will then be evident in your life.

So, how do you seek God's favor? Well, first you must find out where you stand. You must realize that God's favor looks differently than what we would think.

Discern His will and follow it! By doing this, you will automatically walk in his favor.

If you know where you stand, what things do you want Him to give you? If you want an answer to your prayers, then you should be asking how to seek God's reward. If you want an amazing reward for turning your life around, then you should be asking how to seek God's favor. The first thing you need to do when you are praying or trying to turn something around in your life is to find out what it is you want. If you don't know what you want, you won't be able to get it until you figure it out.

Some people have a hard time thinking about what they really want. It might seem like it goes against how prayer works, but this is actually necessary if you want to get a result from prayer. When you are praying, you have to make sure you're focusing on what you really want. Otherwise, you might find yourself not doing anything at all.

Some people don't believe that there's any way that God could help them if they don't ask Him for anything. That might seem like a good idea, but you might be surprised to know that God can actually give you things if you just ask Him for them. Many people don't realize that God might actually send His angels to deliver things instead of people. You might be surprised to know that God might actually send His angel to bring you what you're wanting, instead of just speaking to you about it.

"Therefore, my beloved brethren, be ye stedfast, unmoveable, always abounding in the work of the Lord, forasmuch as ye know that your labour is not in vain in the Lord." - 1 Corinthians 15:58

So, now that you know how to seek God's rewards, how are you going to start doing it? You might think that prayer is the easiest thing to do, but that's not necessarily true. You have to be open to doing what needs to be done for God to show you what you're looking for. If you're not willing to do what it takes, then you won't get what you want from prayer.

If your company is perceived as reliable and can be trusted, it increases the degree of appeal to its customers. Standing in the gap for your people and talking to God about your organization will also determine the extent of good you get from your workplace. Gradually, you will begin to realize that your company is on track, delivering and increasing in productivity & profitability.

Nowadays, it is not strange to find organizations' management in compromising situations to maintain their relevance in the marketplace. In many cases, they may be left with no choice but to give in to the pressures. However, this may take a toll on your stance as an employee and even make you lose your source of income in the long run. See what the Bible says;

"The integrity of the upright will guide them, but the crookedness of the treacherous will destroy them." - Proverbs 11:3 (KJV)

You can change that! You can guide your company and organization aright, and you do not have to be a part of the management team. With prayers, you can change the outlook of things. Peter was in prison after he had been warned not to preach the gospel of Jesus. James had been killed by Herod for doing the same. While in chains, awaiting his execution, unknown to him, his fellow disciples had gathered to pray to God on his behalf for his release. The supernatural intervention of God brought about the eventual release, demonstrating the great power of prayers.

"Therefore when thou doest thine alms, do not sound a trumpet before thee, as the hypocrites do in the synagogues and in the streets, that they may have glory of men. Verily I say unto you, They have their reward." - Matthew 6:2

You need to lift up your voice on behalf of your organization that God should intervene. He will listen because he wants to be involved and glorified in return. *"And I, if I be lifted up from the earth, will draw all men unto me."* John 12:32 (KJV)

PRAYER FOR YOUR ORGANIZATION

Heavenly Father, I pray over the founders/owners of this organization/company that their works may be committed unto you. I pray that they develop a stronger relationship with you.

May their hearts be pliable for you to influence their every move towards the progress of this organization. I pray that they will continually be visionary in all their dealings.

May their vision be ordained and endorsed by you. Order their steps and guide their hands always. Show them the way of righteousness in all of their dealings in Jesus' name. Amen.

REFLECTIONS/NOTES

CHAPTER FIVE

INTERCEDING FOR PEOPLE IN AUTHORITY

"And whatsoever ye do, do it heartily, as to the Lord, and not unto men; knowing that of the Lord, ye shall receive the reward of the inheritance: for ye serve the Lord Christ."

-Colossians 3:23-24

The Bible instructs us to pray for our leaders. This is in no way a way to show that we have expectations from them, irrespective of how good or bad they are. It is a mandate to fulfill His word. Many are fond of criticizing their leaders or other people in positions of authority. God wants us to act like Aaron and Hur, whom God used to lift Moses's arms to conquer the Amalekites. The indication is that they were in support of and have the backing of their leaders.

Of course, our leaders are not supermen. They are men who need our assistance to fulfill their responsibility. Therefore, they need the full and total support of the people they are leading. Also, we have to consider that no leader can singlehandedly fulfill his obligations all by himself; his success is largely dependent on the people around him. It is one thing to buy the vision of the leader and be committed to the cause. It is another to pray for them to succeed because their success is yours, too. We need to pray for them to be endowed with God's wisdom and properly guide the organization to the place they envisioned it to be.

"*If any of you lack wisdom, let him ask of God, that giveth to all men liberally, and upbraideth not; and it shall be given him.*" -James 1:5 (KJV)

Now and then, these leaders are faced with various scenarios within and without the organization that determines their success. With God's wisdom, they will be able to discern situations properly and resolve them in the best possible way. Now, this is only achievable if men are lifting up their hands in prayer on their behalf. When you cultivate the habit of lifting your superiors up to God in prayer, you show that you are interested in their success, extending to your colleagues and subordinates. Irrespective of the kind of person he or she is, interceding for him will encourage him to be kind, gentle, and faithful to the cause. The scriptures tell us in *1 Timothy 2:1-3 (KJV)*,

"I exhort therefore, that, first of all, supplications, prayers, intercessions, and giving of thanks, be made for all men; For kings, and for all that are in authority; that we may lead a quiet and peaceable life in all godliness and honesty. For this is good and acceptable in the sight of God our Savior;"

One of your roles as a Christian in your workplace is to pray for people in authority. Their success is your success. Their win is yours too. If they fail, you may partake of the same. Pray that God grants them the spirit and strength to live according to His will. Paul admonished us to continually pray for our leaders till we see the manifestation of the Christ kind of life in them. *"My little children, of whom I travail in birth again until Christ be formed in you."* Galatians 4:19 (KJV).

PRAYER FOR YOUR SUPERVISORS

Father, I thank you for the leadership of my organization and my supervisors. Thank you for what you have yet done in their lives and their leadership position. I pray that even as they continually lead in this organization, your wisdom shall be at work in them and at every point. They shall exhibit the character of Christ in their activities and in all they do in Jesus' name. Amen.

REFLECTIONS/NOTES

CHAPTER SIX
INTERCEDING FOR YOUR COWORKERS

"And the second is like, namely this, 'Thou shalt love thy neighbor as yourself.' There is no other commandment greater than these."

- Mark 12:31 *(KJV)*

As humans, we are all running a different and individual race in life. While it is unnecessary to see your colleagues and coworkers as competition, the goal is to be the best you can be wherever you find yourself. Remember, you were employed based on your skills, peculiarities, and capabilities, not because you had similar traits to another person. This is why you don't need to compete with anyone in your workplace, especially with how you relate and associate with others. In essence, try to keep an open mind towards your coworkers. Be happy for them when they are promoted and show empathy where and when necessary.

In Romans 12:15 (KJV), God's word says, "*Rejoice with them that do rejoice, and weep with them that weep.*"

God's desire is for us to be our brothers' keepers and look out for people around us. How do you do that? There are many ways. One of these ways is to lend them a helping hand by praying for them. You can be a leaning shoulder to bear some burdens when necessary. You need to be able to pray for your colleague(s) because a win for one is a win for all, given the company's goal as a functional organization comprising of different people. Ask God to open their eyes to see the wrong they are committing lest they continue with that until they are ruined. Cultivate the habit of praying to God to touch your colleagues' hearts and change the hearts of those who are misbehaving. A selfless believer will not wait until his friend or coworker is destroyed before he or she acts. As much as you go to God for your personal requests, you can also help others in the place of prayer like we see in the Bible:

"And I sought for a man among them, that should make up the hedge, and stand in the gap before me for the land..." - Ezekiel 22:30 (KJV)

God wants us to rise up on behalf of others in times of need and help channel them in the right direction with the help of the Holy Spirit. Prayer is an instrumental key to the success of an organization. Before a coworker commits a blunder and is probably set up for retrenchment, interceding before God by standing in the gap for them is much more effective.

PRAYER FOR COWORKERS

Father, thank you for the life of every one of my fellow workers. Thank you for their current position in this organization.

I pray, Father, that you continually show them your mercy in all that they do. I pray, Father, that you cause your love to flourish in their heart, and you guide them in their everyday activities in Jesus' name.

Save them from errors and teach them with your Spirit to excel in their respective endeavors. Amen.

REFLECTIONS/NOTES

CHAPTER SEVEN
MAINTAINING ETHICS IN THE MARKETPLACE

"And let us consider to one another to provoke unto love and to good works; not forsaking the assembling of ourselves together, as the manner of some is; but exhorting one another; and so much the more, as ye see the day approaching."

- Hebrews 10:24-25 *(KJV)*

Christian Faith in the marketplace defines the extent of ethics and values upheld. Generally speaking, lack of practicality of spirituality can jeopardize an individual's desire to follow the respective given ethics. In other words, it is not convenient to simply "want to follow" the ethics and guiding principles. Something must inspire you to do. Thus, your profession of faith in Christ and spirituality will go a long way in helping you achieve this. This is why you need to be more practical, especially with prayers. First, one of your key duties is to live a life that directly and indirectly encourages others to take ethical actions and decisions to spur the marketplace's excellence. Cultivate the habit of praying for your friends, coworkers, and the sustainability and/or prosperity of your organization at all times.

Your job as a follower of Christ is to be actively interested in others' affairs and, more importantly, their well-being. That is one way to hold moral and organizational ethics firmly. As Christ would, you must be pragmatic about having the interest of others at heart.

"Let nothing be done through strife or vainglory; but in lowliness of mind let each esteem other better than themselves." Philippians 2:3 *(KJV)*

When we desire to serve others, particularly putting their needs above and beyond our self-interests and growth, it means we are interested in fostering ethics in the marketplace. Because we are Christians, we have the grace of God to achieve this feat. You, therefore, must want to make grace available to others to enjoy, too. This, I believe, is the true essence of ethics.

As implied by Paul, true faith in Christ generally increases our love for our friends, colleagues, and other persons. It basically gives us hope in this life and the one to come where our priorities and perspectives are changed. Now that we know what is important, which is to love all, and not just those in our inner circle of relationships, this hope in Christ is critical to our wellness, both mentally and emotionally. It helps us ease off worry, stress, anxiety and, consequently, instill perseverance and determination to keep going even when tough.

Bringing up another to that realm of hope will simultaneously result in the stirring of their faith, and such that in the long run, there is really no need to address ethical issues in the marketplace because faith, love, and hope will be the lifestyle, and these would go on to ensure that we bear fruits, and live the lives that are "worthy of the Lord." In essence, genuine faith will produce changes in how we think, speak and act as Christ-followers. "*For the hope which is laid up for you in heaven, whereof ye heard before in the word of the truth of the gospel; which is come unto you, as it is in all the world; and bringeth forth fruit, as it doth also in you, since the day ye heard of it, and knew the grace of God in truth."* Colossians 1:5-6 (KJV).

Virtues are major ingredients of ethics and are critical to Christian living. To get the best of it, we should ask in prayer for God to strengthen us and increase our faith in Him. We cannot merely believe things like spiritual wisdom, trusting the power of God to be patient and have joyful endurance, or demonstrate hope, faith, and love. It is utterly essential to pray about these things and seek God's face to empower us. Have you ever thought of how crucial and helpful it would be to pray that God bestows on someone (your colleagues, employers, and others in the marketplace) - the patience and endurance they need to overcome the trials and temptations without giving up hope?

As a Christian, you have the authority in Christ's name to do this, and all we need is to harness the special grace to make the world a better place. You have been strategically placed in the marketplace in this season and time for a particular reason. I believe the purpose of having you on that job is to influence some laid-down principles to suit the organization's ethical standards. You have authority over everything on earth, above it, and beneath. Therefore, whatever you bind here on earth, it's bound in heaven in Christ's name, and the things you loose are loosed by the blood of Jesus. As a joint heir with Christ, you are expected to flourish in attitudes, morals, and otherwise. You must break forth in all directions, and this should manifest in your business affairs, as it infects others, too. Therefore, it is high time you began taking charge and commanding the power, principality, and ruler of darkness to let go of the space because you carry the light of God.

Ethics and Christianity are indeed inseparable, except we do not want to tell ourselves the truth. Therefore, with the God-given power to possess the land and influence the system, agency, and entire marketplace, you have a heritage from God that others must benefit from to achieve a unified goal.

Moreover, there are other things you can do to help your marketplace commit to its ethical standards. Part of this is to use the Bible as a tool to change the values of your organization. You can use your Christian influence to help bring your colleagues and coworkers into harmonious consensus about a subject. As a consequence, you will inevitably navigate your way to the top in your professional endeavor successfully. So, very precisely, the message is about endeavoring to apply the Christian values and practices you have mastered and learned in Christianity to your marketplace to help you win favor from God and attain the seemingly impossible height. However, you must help others develop their faith in God to live according to God's plans for their lives. More certainly, make efforts to apply the Biblical business principles of money and decision-making to influence our marketplace's ethical principles. This cannot be achieved merely by talking to people or impacting them with your values alone. You need to do more with prayer, and you certainly need the help of the Holy Spirit.

PRAYER FOR UPHOLDING ETHICS:

Thank you, God, for the faith you have given us in Christ to love all and have our hope laid up in heaven. Thank you for the word of truth, for the light you have shown us again. Thank you for the wisdom you have granted us to understand the role of upholding organizational ethics and not just for ourselves but for all.

We ask that you help us bear more fruits and grow, fill us with the knowledge of YOUR will to understand all things, and grow in wisdom, so that we may lead lives worthy of the Christian race. Help us to be strong with your power, and prepare us to endure everything patiently as we share the inheritance of this grace with the saints. We have redemption in your name, and our sins are forgiven. Henceforth, we take charge of the affairs of the marketplace from the spiritual realm. We no longer have ethic-related issues as we are drawn closer to you and become like you in our thoughts and actions.

Thank you for the special grace released unto us; we ask and receive in your name. Amen!

REFLECTIONS/NOTES

CHAPTER EIGHT
COMPETITION IN MARKETPLACE

"Know ye not that they which run in a race run all, but on receiveth the prize? So run, that ye may obtain. And every man that striveth for the mastery is temperate in all things. Now they do it to obtain a corruptible crown; but we an incorruptible. I therefore so run, not as uncertainly; so, fight I, not as one that beateth the air: But I keep under my body, and bring it into subjection: lest that by any means, when I have preached to others, I myself should be a castaway."

- 1 Corinthians 9:24-27 *(KJV)*

There is a bubbling question among Christians on whether competition is healthy and Christianly in the marketplace. Perhaps you are among the many wrestling with the same thought. You can find an answer in this chapter. For some of us who are entrepreneurs and consider whether competition is a dirty word, I believe competition is necessary.

I would say that it is okay to feel that it might be ungodly and that it might be strategically about greed and getting what you want at the expense of others. It is, or in some cases, can be like that. After all, competition is considered ungodly and unhealthy when it brings about the destruction of another's business or way of life in the marketplace.

Whether in business or other things, the Christian perspective on competition may seem like the drive to be the best, which ultimately may not be in line with humbling oneself and serving God as we ought. But competition is an intrinsic part of a business that makes the world go round. In a way or another, you must have competed against other agencies in your respective industry, and maybe sometimes you won and lost on another. Wherever the luck must have fallen, it is not necessary to take it personally. But, then, it is not strange to find that Christians are somewhat squeamish about competition as of today.

We can retain our Christianity in a competitive marketplace by taking it to God in prayer. Pray that God helps our weaknesses and helps us with His spirit- to act, think and behave rightly according to His will. I mean, it is not enough to merely get over the feeling that competition might indeed be necessary or appropriate. How you handle the situation matters too.

Biblically, Apostle Paul merited this view when he talked about running and winning the race. He did not particularly discard competition from God's orbit. Winning a race may seem more appealing, but there is an element of competition required in the real sense. However, it must be done right as a part of being a functioning person. This makes me wonder what life would be like without competition.

Competition in the marketplace is a strategic way of bringing out the best of us and helping our organizations maintain an edge above others in knowledge, practice, and handling problems. Although competition can be win-win in some cases where businesses can pull together and develop winning solidarity. Still, competition with a handful of ethics is what I am talking about here. This might be part of the driving force to the requisite sense of identity and worth to excel in the marketplace. Contrarily, unfettered competition may be truly brutal as many consider it to be. Thus, the positive theology of competitive behavior is built on the frameworks of prayer to achieve our specific business and organizational goals.

So, what should we do as Christians? First, we must strive to do our job the best and legitimate way we can wherever we find ourselves. Having a relationship with God requires us to be faithful in our walk with Him. *"And whatsoever ye do, do it heartily, as to the Lord, and not unto men; Knowing that of the Lord ye shall receive the reward of the inheritance for ye serve the Lord Christ."* Colossians 3:23-24 *(KJV)*

The support of competition by the Bible is evidenced in the opening passage of this chapter. The emphasis is that not everyone involved in a race/business/project (participants) will end up with the crown of victory. To get to the finish line, you want to make every punch count, such that you are not left behind in the race or even disqualified in the long run. However, considering this same passage in the typical Christian life would mean that the prizes we are to win must be eternal, which does not contribute to the shortage of heavenly treasure. That is, in actuality, our rewards are largely based on our striving to attain spiritual excellence by assisting others in the body of Christ.

The standard in the kingdom is when our sister and brothers win, we win. Bringing this to perspective, in the marketplace, identifying competition as part of the business is important. Then, figuring out who the competitors are should not be to spite or disrepute their works. Rather, it should be to ensure that your win and that of your entire organization is godly and not at the expense of anyone's wins.

This is where Paul's admonition in 1 Corinthians 15:58 becomes handy, *"Therefore, my beloved brethren, be ye steadfast, unmoveable, always abounding in the work of the Lord, for as much as ye know that your labour is not in vain in the Lord."*

Clearly, rewarding motivation is a major factor in living the ideal and optimal Christian life. Still, the strive for excellence may not necessarily connote competition or succeeding at the expense of others. It is the opposite. Do not relax, living on the assumptions that there may not be competition amongst believers in the marketplace here on earth. Yes, it is great to lend our fellow a hand up. But you will not, in the name of being a Christian, allow anyone to pull you down. This would result in living below the purpose of God for your life, and in the long run, you may even not get the eventual prize of the eternal crown. Take a look at Paul's comment in the passage;

"I press toward the mark for the prize of the high calling of God in Christ Jesus." -Philippians 3:14 (KJV). Paul's "pressing" clarifies that the effort in what we tag competition is not the problem. The effort is necessary to indicate that we are serving an excellent God- one who does not condone mediocrity. Meanwhile, we must beware of the element of selfishness inherent, which makes us seek advantage, glory for ourselves, and attention that is not concerned with our fellow brothers and sisters' spiritual welfare in the Lord. More precisely, the idea is to help one another achieve the rewards we seek, and that way, we can get ours, too. *"...doth not behave itself unseemly, seeketh not her own, is not easily provoked, thinketh no evil."* -1 Corinthians 13:5 (KJV)

Therefore, we can conclude that the "spirit" of competition, especially in the marketplace, is a good thing when directed and applied properly. As we strive to do our best to maintain the Christian life, our fellow Christians in the marketplace can enjoy the benefits as well, thanks to our efforts, of course, not to our self-glory. This is the only time competition in the marketplace is healthy and godly. The ultimate should be our focus and in the sense of what Ecclesiastes 4:4 records, that, "*Again, I considered all travail, and every right work, that for this a man is envied of his neighbor. This is also vanity and vexation of spirit.*"

Nonetheless, from God's perspective, the overall idea is that why we do something is just as important as what we do. Apostle Paul gives a clear picture of dealing with competition as a Christian in his letter to the church in Corinth. He challenges us to do more than run the race for the sake of it, but that we should run to win. "*I have fought the good fight, I have finished the race, I have kept the faith.*" -2 Timothy 4:7 (KJV)

To run a race means you want to run with other people, and when you do so with the best, you become better yourself. Thus, we can sharpen one another through competition. Therefore, our goal in competing should be in two-folds:

I. To use our God-given talents and gifts to the best of our abilities and,
II. To win in the marketplace, competing in hopes of prospering yourself, colleagues and others, NOT directly at the expense of others.

In the marketplace, think of competition as: to give up the ability and talent would be to hold God in contempt, and to win is to honor Him.

Our desire to compete and win should not be for our own selfish interests but to honor God. This is why the attitude and motivation in our hearts are all that matters. In my study and research, I have found that competition can be useful in our race, and it can help us maximize our return to our maker. Competition can foster excellence and direct us to focus on areas of work where we can effectively maximize our passion. It can also enhance the participants' performance and not just the winners.

You see why it is important to allow competition in the marketplace? In fact, there is nothing you can do about it but admit that it is real. Its existence should rather be embraced and tailored to your success and that of your organization.

However, keep in mind that your opponent in the industry is not your adversary. In actuality, you are not competing against him. Competition is necessary to help us become what God wants us to be. Thus, our faithfulness is what pleases and honors Him. This is why I cannot overemphasize the need to steward your talents, skills, and Christianity for God's glory as well as the good of others. In a nutshell, a competitive marketplace established under God's sovereignty will help us love our neighbors better. That way, we can provide better services for the blessing of humanity. Therefore, a Christian would bring God's hands into the marketplace where he or she serves through prayer.

With God, winning and losing will only be taken as occasions to sanctify and strengthen ourselves- so that we can both be conscious of our fallibility as sinners and to deploy our talents more effectively. I implore you to do all things as unto the Lord. When you do not attach your value to those you outperform, you will enjoy the peace of healthy competition in your marketplace. Speak to God to help your weakness, and that going forward, you want to have a fruitful relationship in your marketplace. Also, understand that you need God's wisdom to direct you to learn the acts of living with competition and not compromising your faith in the process.

PRAYER FOR COMBATING COMPETITION

Thank you, Father, for the benefits of the friends and competition you have placed in my life and relationship to develop in my journey on earth. I am indeed grateful for the relationships in my marketplace that I enjoy and thrive in today and the joys that each of them brings in their own unique way.

Father, I thank you for giving me the grace to learn and know the truth about competition. I have been doing it the wrong way so far; please show me mercy. Father Lord, I pray that you help me and the entire staff of my organization demonstrate absolute steadfastness in your word and faith in you that you alone can help us abound in you. Our labor will not be in vain. Today, we receive special grace to be the best in the marketplace, and we will not force it. You, Lord, will make it happen your own way. I pray that I will not take these relationships for granted. I will no longer strive to reap at their expense, but I will increase in value for each of them. By your power, I will build up and strengthen others in the bonds of love and peace. These relationships will bring me increased fruitfulness, as they are founded on your love and blessings. Amen!

REFLECTIONS/NOTES

CHAPTER NINE

MANIFESTATION OF GOD'S GLORY

"For God, who commanded the light to shine out of darkness, hath shined in our hearts, to give the light of the knowledge of the glory of God in the face of Jesus Christ."

– 2 Corinthians 4:6 (KJV)

Moses became a carrier of God's glory after spending time with God on Mount Sinai. Forty days and forty nights was all the time it took. In the same vein, the glory of God is accessible to all, with equal right to partake of the same at any given time. Meanwhile, our readiness to commit the entirety of our lives to God is the only differentiating factor. For instance, an individual who spends so much time with God- communing with Him and enjoying his presence- cannot have the same results as one who does only sparingly. God is no respecter of any man. He will give His time and attention to the individual who devotes more time daily to know Him. He will certainly not hold back His promises, neither will He make his ways unknown to such person. You must cultivate the habit of spending time with God to experience His might in your workplace environment, in the lives of your supervisors/managers, and that of your co-workers. Being consistent in your daily walk with God will ultimately ensure that you always have the plethora of God's glory around you.

The manifestation of God's glory in the earth is not a matter of faith but relies on perfect obedience. Many have claimed to have received revelations concerning the coming of the Holy Ghost and the appearance of Jesus Christ. Some have received their revelations as a dream or as an inner voice. In other instances, God has used the manifestation of God's glory in the earth to accomplish works of mercy and compassion.

There is much truth in this claim. We have been given revelation concerning the ways of God. Revelation is how we learn more about God and His purposes for His people. Revelation helps us understand the future. It reveals to us what things are to come and when. It also teaches us what to expect so that we can be ready when the time comes.

The Bible contains many verses that speak about the coming of the Redeemer. There are also several references to His existence in the Old Testament. There are references to His existence as far back as Genesis. There is a mention of Him in the New Testament. Finally, the Bible indicates that He lives and reigns in Heaven. In these scriptures, we find a clear indication of His presence and the coming of His Kingdom.

Through the Word of God, we get a glimpse into the future. Revelation shows us the things that will happen in the future. Revelation gives us insight into the thoughts and intents of God. Revelation shows us what will be. Revelation's goal is our understanding of all these things. This is why we have the imperative need for a revelation to enter into the promises of God.

"Who being the brightness of [his] glory, and the express image of his person, and upholding all things by the word of his power, when he had by himself purged our sins, sat down on the right hand of the Majesty on high" - **Hebrews 1:3**

This secret word is revealed for our advantage. Revelation helps us build on our strengths and use our weaknesses for a purpose. If we know what God's plan is for us and if we are willing to accept His promises, then we will never go wrong.

God's secret word is not an abstract book or treatise that has been written by men, but it is God's promise to mankind. It is God's plan for our redemption. It is God's will for our healing and restoration. It is the will of the Most High, and it is up to us to turn it around and use it to our advantage.

Revelation shows us that there is a power bigger than ourselves, which controls all things. We are told that if we want to see great things, we should go to where they are. Revelation helps us do just that.

That is what a manifestation is. It is the opening up of the secret word of God for our salvation. We cannot walk by this promise without the help of this secret word. We cannot walk through the door of the Kingdom of God without the help of revelation. This is the reason that Pentacles are placed in prominent positions throughout the Bible.

We can only imagine how wonderful it will be when the secret word of God is revealed. When the Kingdom of God is revealed, we will see the King of glory, the Lord Jesus. We will sit down with him, and with our lips, he will teach us everything we need to know. We will never again be in the dark regarding His ways and His purposes.

We can understand that He is the ONE who created and is the ONE who is in charge. We are told that when He comes back, He will show us His glory. We are told that when He comes back, there will be an utterance like that of thunder. We will have an appearance like that of the blind. We will be shown the path of eternal life.

That is what a manifestation is. It is the revealing of God's glory. It is God speaking to us. It is the perfect example of the way.

I would submit to you that there is absolutely nothing that a believer could know or understand that the average Christian does not know without training and experience. Revelation is a private experience between the revealed God and the individual who is bold enough to receive the revelation. You may disagree with me on this. You may even say that I don't have a clear enough view of what is revealed.

The Bible says God cannot be fooled. To experience an outpour of the release of God's glory in your workplace, you have to put in the work and give it what it takes. Given the equal opportunity available to all to come to Him and draw as much as we want, our commitment to His words and consistency in walking with Him defines how much of His glory we will encounter.

We are told in the scriptures that *"Peter fairly exploded with his good news: "It's God's own truth, nothing could be plainer: God plays no favorites!"- Act 10:34 (MSG)*

Your marketplace should be an environment where agape love is required to achieve common objectives; no matter what they are, we cannot behave like the world. For instance, rising at the expense of another's downfall in your marketplace indicates toxicity. God does not want this. His glory cannot thrive in such an atmosphere. Although everyone has a role to play when it comes to experiencing the glory of God, its realization and ultimate release can begin when our heart is set for its manifestation.

The glory of God goes beyond a mere divine energy force floating in the marketplace in some mystical manner. It is His character and divine nature – also called the essence of God's presence. God's glory is requisite to prosper and thrive in whatever we set our hearts to and wherever we find ourselves. The Bible says Jesus is the perfect revelation of the Glory of God. *"The Son is the radiance of God's glory and the exact representation of his being, sustaining all things by his powerful word."* -Hebrews 1:3 (NIV)

First, you have to understand the importance of seeking God's glory- that it can make a lot of things different, especially bringing about an environment where peace, love, joy, abundance, and other good things are sustained. You can then talk to God about the release of the glory before talking to your co-workers and supervisors about the necessity. By the time you take this matter to them, you are confident that it is not the words you speak that thrill them. It is not how beautifully you were able to present it, but because your words now carry the breath and power of God. At this time, you have the assurance that their response would be positive. Let God take it from there and do what He can do.

"And it came to pass, when Moses came down from mount Sinai with the two tables of testimony in Moses' hand, when he came down from the mount, that Moses wist not that the skin of his face shone while he talked with him. And when Aaron and all the children of Israel saw Moses, behold, the skin of his face shone; and they were afraid to come nigh him."- Exodus 34:29-30 (KJV)

The glory of God is within reach, and you can take as much as you want from it for your personal and organizational benefits - including a God-present marketplace environment.

REFLECTIONS/NOTES

CHAPTER TEN

COMMANDING GOD'S FAVOR

"And the Lord gave the people favor in the sight of the Egyptians, so that they lent unto them such things as they required. And they spoiled the Egyptians."

– Exodus 12:36 (KJV)

The Lord favored the Israelites, and this made their journey out of Egypt and to the land of Canaan particularly seamless. Also, Joseph enjoyed God's unlimited favor in His life. For instance, while in the house of Potiphar, God's favor was undeniably evident all through his sojourn, and he was ultimately able to fulfill his destiny.

Perhaps the whole nation of Egypt would have been ruined by famine and hunger had Joseph not enjoyed God's favor. Invariably, Egypt was preserved because a man favored by God was among them. The same applies to you, too. You carry the power of God to seek and cause the release of His favor on your workplace. The outcome of which would be tremendous for you and the organization as a whole.

Everyone can be a partaker of God's favor. When you are favored by God, you have the duty of bringing about its release in your workplace. You are a beneficiary of this special ability. Ephesians 1:11 says, *"In him we have obtained an inheritance, having been predestined according to the purpose of him who works all things according to the counsel of his will."*

Often, we tend to ignore or shove aside specific instructions that could solve the problems we encounter here and there in life. Many have deliberately withheld God's solution to solve their workplace challenges. As a child of God, you are a problem-solver. You should be willing to demonstrate how valuable you are at all times, especially to the growth of your organization. *"For the earnest expectation of the creature waiteth for the manifestation of the sons of God."* - Romans 8:19 (KJV)

Put the God-given blessing of His favor to use will inevitably increase His blessings upon you when you heed his instructions and follow in total obedience. The parable of the master and his servants explains this even better. You don't have to act like the third servant. Learn from the first two servants and Joseph.

Make use of your God-given gift of being the favored of the Lord to profit all.

REFLECTIONS/NOTES

CHAPTER ELEVEN
PRAYING FOR PROMOTION

"For promotion cometh neither from the east, nor from the west, nor from the south."

- Psalm 75:6 (KJV)

Leadership is a position of influence. You do not need to be in the place of authority to influence, impact or add value. In fact, it's high time you evolved from being a V.I.P (Very Important Person) to a V.A.P (Value Adding Person). A problem solved indicates added value, and when value is added, your importance is recognized and rewarded.

However, promotion and increase should not be in the front line of what you seek. Of course, God wants us to live a good life and advance in life, but it shouldn't be our do-or-die ambition. Look at what the Bible says in Proverbs 4:18 (KJV), *"But the path of the just is as the shining light, that shineth more and more unto the perfect day."* He cares for you more than you can imagine, and He is surely going to lift us up beyond our very imagination.

We must bear in mind that God's plans for us are good and not evil. God desires for us to walk in authority, honor, and great stature in the earth realm. As we understand this, we conclude that God wants us to prosper, and if he wants us to prosper, he will surely guide and direct us in the way we should go. In the workplace, we can be overwhelmed by the great desire to climb the corporate ladder, and it becomes the thing that we strive for day and night. We give it our full attention until it eventually consumes us.

Often this causes us to do things that are not right before God. We display a level of desperation for the next level until we are willing to mishandle our coworkers and colleagues. We are willing to damage friendships and work relationships, ultimately bringing total chaos to our working environment. We have to come to the place where we understand. Matthew 6:33 is the key… *Seek first the Kingdom of God and His righteousness, and everything else shall be added to you.* Suppose we would get in the mindset of seeking first the Lord and his righteousness. In that case, everything else will be added to us, including promotion. Our greatest desire should always be to put God first in every aspect of our life. It should never be a position or a salary, an influence or title. It should always be God. You can cultivate such an atmosphere by the way you conduct yourself personally. Your attitude of righteousness will become contagious in your workplace through the words you speak through the wisdom you bestow, and even your mannerism. You have a personal responsibility to maintain the righteousness of God in your workplace as a believer. Never allow the greed for the next level to overcome you; it creates a toxic working environment. In a toxic work environment, men are always willing to destroy one another to get the lead on them. This is exhausting behavior and mindset, which will cause you to eventually burn out or react more destructively as this level of evilness persists.

Humility before the Lord

James 4:10 tells us to humble ourselves before the Lord, and he will exalt us. Humility is the way up. It may not sound like or even feel like the fashionable thing to do in a workplace; however, promotion does not come from men; it comes from God. Humility brings forth promotion. God can call your name from the back to the front. He can set your face on the heart of men. He can give you unmeasurable favor even with those who do not prefer you. Learning to walk in a greater level of humility before God and man should be one of our greatest goals.

Where there is humility, honor will be bestowed. In Matthew 23:11-12, Jesus said the greatest among you must be a servant, but those who exalt themselves will be humbled. Those who humble themselves will be exalted. This is a spiritual principle and concept that the carnal man struggles to understand. If we look at the life of Jesus, though he was the greatest man to walk the earth, he yet came as a servant, and his selfless sacrifice upon the cross is still serving us today.

Do not waste your time crafting a plan to advance the ladder of greatness for many are the plans of man, but in the end, it is the purpose of the Lord that shall prevail. The Lord shall place upon whom he will honor and promote. Fix your mind on becoming a servant serving to your best ability. This requires great humility. Often a servant will not receive the accolades in which they so desire. Servants must serve under people who are not as kind and compassionate as they should be. True servants always put others first regardless of their level of qualification. True servants right their wrongs. They are not arrogant and bullheaded. They are tender-hearted, willing to apologize and repent whether they feel they are wrong or not. True servants take responsibility and are always willing to put in the extra work whenever necessary. The Unsolicited willingness to go above and beyond rest at the heart of a true servant. True servants are those who walked in humility humble are the true servants.

Trust that the Lord will cause the right eyes to see you working in the field at its appropriate time. You do not have to belittle or expose anyone to be seen. If we will bear in mind that putting out someone else's light will never cause our light to shine brighter, it is when we are willing to help someone else's light to shine that our light shines brighter.

PRAYER FOR PROMOTION AND INCREASE

Father, I thank you because you always answer my prayers. Thank you for the opportunity to serve and add value to my workplace. I come to you that you grant me the revelation of your true self and prune me of any negative motives in my desire to attain promotion.

Help me to constantly bear in mind that only you can promote and increase me. Father, give me the grace to wait until the time is right for me to be promoted. Also, Lord, please give my supervisors and co-workers the same mind of waiting for your time so that we all can enjoy your peace in our workplace. Amen.

REFLECTIONS/NOTES

CHAPTER TWELVE
EFFECTIVE PRAYER LIST FOR THE MARKETPLACE

We have come to the final chapter of this book. Please endeavor to say these prayers. The goal is to experience God's hand and the manifestation of His presence in our lives, the lives of our supervisors, co-workers, and ensure that we have all-around success in the marketplace.

- Father, we thank you for our organization. Thank you for making the idea of our founders a reality.
- Father, we thank you for the birthing of our organization. Thank you because regardless of where we are right now, we are headed for the top.
- Father, we thank you for how far you have brought our organization, thank you for our leaders, thank you for the wisdom that has brought us this far.

- Father, we thank you for every employee in this organization. Thank you for their lives, families and for preserving them.
- Father, we thank you for every employee in our organization, thank you for their conformation to your will and character.
- Father, we pray that every one of our leaders shall not compromise their values and standards for negative standards and values in Jesus' name.
- Father, we pray that our leaders shall uphold their integrity at every point in time in Jesus' name.
- Father, we pray that our leaders shall continually lead our organization right in each of our activities in Jesus' name.
- Father, we pray that our organization continually experiences favor in every area of operations in Jesus' name.
- Father, we pray that our organization would not deal with wrong individuals that would tarnish our organization's image in Jesus' name.

- Father, we pray that our organization shall not employ the wrong individuals to bring shame to our organization in Jesus' name.
- Father, we pray that every one of our supervisors exhibits the God kind of character in all their dealings in Jesus' name.
- Father, we always pray that our organization shall continually acknowledge you in every one of their ways in Jesus' name.
- Father, we pray that every co-worker in our organization exhibits the Godly kind of character at all times in Jesus' name.
- Father, we pray that your love reigns in the hearts of every staff of our organization at all times in Jesus' name.
- Father, we pray that unity reigns in our organization at all times in Jesus' name.
- Father, we pray that you prune the hearts of every staff of our organization that we have the right motives at all times in Jesus' name.
- Father, we pray that you continually lead our organization to make exponential progress every year in Jesus' name.

✝ Father, we pray that the character of Christ shall be exhibited by them in all they do in Jesus' name.

REFLECTIONS/NOTES

ABOUT THE AUTHOR
NORI MOORE

Conference speaker, revivalist, pastoral counselor, and mentor Nori Moore is a woman after God's own heart, seeking to lead the people of God by providing strategies and tools to empower the church to be efficient in the ministry of prayer, intercession, and deliverance. She currently serves in the Body of Christ as an Apostle in The Lord's Church.

At the age of 19, Apostle Nori gave her life to the Lord under Pastor Author L. Brown's leadership at Rosedale First Born Church. Through many trials and tribulations, she has found her purpose in the Most High God to serve his people in love and intercession. Her passion for God and surrendered lifestyle have led to anointing to pray, preach, and teach the Word of God with authority, revelation, and deliverance.

Today, Apostle Nori is the proud and devoted founder of Emmanuel Global Ministries, with locations in various cities. Using her expertise in Anger

Management and Christian Spiritual Counseling, Apostle Nori and her ministry effectively deal with the reality of Christian issues calling for true deliverance and unmasking. She develops prayer, intercessory prayer training materials, and other media to provide sound teaching and guidance for the 21st-century church.

When she's not running her ministry, Apostle Nori serves the Lord as an inspirational, thought-provoking evangelical speaker, delivering messages that inspire, encourage, and bring effective change in the lives of those who embrace the Word of God. She also enjoys spending quality time with her husband and six handsome young sons in their hometown of Tallahassee, Florida.

www.ingramcontent.com/pod-product-compliance
Lightning Source LLC
Chambersburg PA
CBHW071141090426
42736CB00012B/2196